THE BUTTERFLY TOUCH

Recovery
Through Poetry

Dessa Byrd Reed

THE BUTTERFLY TOUCH
RECOVERY THROUGH POETRY

Deer Publishing
PMB 164
74924 Country Club Drive #150
Palm Desert, Ca. 92260

Grateful acknowledgment is made to
jc west for original watercolor used on the cover

Cover design by Robert Howard

Printed   02 01 00   ♥   10 9 8 7 6 5 4 3 2 1

Library of Congress Card Number: 00-190689

Publisher's Cataloging-in-Publication

(Provided by Quality Books, Inc.)

Reed, Dessa Byrd.
    The butterfly touch : recovery through poetry /
Dessa Byrd Reed. -- 1st ed.
    p. cm.
    ISBN: 0-9678767-3-7

    1. Healing--Poetry.   I. Title

PS3568.E364825B88 2000   811'.6
                     QBI00-241

ACKNOWLEDGEMENTS

I am grateful to The Rancho Mirage, California, Public Library Poetry Group, especially Dorothea Bisbas, workshop leader. They have given me tremendous support in learning to write and appreciate poetry. The opportunity to critique each other's creative work is a significant benefit.

Thanks to Jan Castro (aka jc west) who first suggested I record my thoughts in a journal. She also captured my idea for the cover in an original watercolor.

My forever friends, Shannon and Scott Peck, encouraged me greatly, and both were extremely helpful in the editing and publishing. They have my deep love and appreciation.

All those who took part in my physical care and comfort have a special place in my heart.

I feel like an actor receiving an Oscar -- I want to thank everyone I have ever known.

I want to thank....

To my daughter
Kathy
You hold the Olympic gold
for your
BUTTERFLY TOUCH

TABLE OF CONTENTS

A PERSONAL TOUCH

In 1997, I was in a serious automobile accident. I feel that the years of building a spiritual foundation had a great deal to do with my survival.

During months of recovery and healing, I began to write down some of my deepest insights. These jottings soon started to rhyme, and I realized a poem was being born.

At that time, I knew little about poetry. I did realize, however, that writing poems gave me tremendous satisfaction. With each new attempt, I seemed to close a wound, both physically and emotionally. Delight replaced depression.

Then I began to attend a poetry critique group at our local library. Their kindness and expertise were encouraging to me. I learned to write free verse and began to soar with this freedom. I also learned a lot about humility. It was not easy to have my infant verse critiqued -- even when they were right!

Now the poetry flows. It is like studying a new language and then thinking in it. I think in poetry. I have tried to develop the craft of verse writing using metaphors to create images or imply a message. Understanding terms like alliteration, epiphany, enjambment, oxymoron, and iambic pentameter are helpful, but not essential to unlocking the treasures within.

I don't know all the technical rules of the various meters, but that is not the point of this book. My motive is to help others find healing through their poetic voice and the fulfillment that comes with this discovery. We all have it as a part of our expression of life. It is not a *how to* but a *you can* book.

Age has nothing to do with this art form. I have spoken to first graders, high school students, and many retirees. Even their first attempts were amazing.

Your ideas expressed in poetry will make you feel creative, esteemed, and just plain happy, whether anyone reads it or not. You will probably begin to see things you never noticed before, or remember incidents long forgotten. These will inspire you to write.

My story of recovery is written in both prose and poetry. It takes courage to open so private an experience to the world, but I feel it will be helpful to those in recovery of any kind -- injury, illness, grief, substance abuse or whatever. Perhaps the need is just more creativity in your life.

The poems are arranged by topics. There is a page at the end of each section to encourage *you* to write your own poem. This is my gift to you. We all have resistance. Look at the one entitled, "Discovering the Poet Within," which shows mine. When you finish this book, I hope you will have written a poem you might even want to share.

Poetry is conquering the world,
let us surrender to this creative Power.

Dessa Byrd Reed

TOUCHED

BY

THE

MOMENT

We live in moments. On one of my dark days several weeks after the accident, a friend suggested I write down some of my random thoughts. She is an artist and poet, who always carries a small spiral notebook in which she can sketch or write at the moment of inspiration.

I bought the loveliest journal I could find – green with a white orchid on the cover. I was sure that the prettier the notebook, the better I would write. At least it made me feel a tiny bit professional. I timidly began to record some of my inspiration, even sketch a bit. At first I felt foolish, especially when I drew a tree or a bird – or wrote a poem that I knew was contrived.

I vowed no one would see my early efforts. I treated it like a diary – totally confidential. My journal soon became part of my anatomy and went with me everywhere. What a difference that small gesture did for my outlook!

Over the months I moved from bed to wheelchair to walker to cane to walking again. The greatest lesson I learned during that time was to live in the moment. As I wrote and prayed, I decided to live only in the NOW, no regrets of the past or dread of the future. Writing positive poetry about everyday experiences often dispelled the darkness. The more I wrote, the better the writing. I even began to like my own poetry and to share it with others.

The
following poems
capture
a few butterfly moments.

THE BUTTERFLY TOUCH

How gently the butterfly makes its rounds,
touching each leaf with no harsh sounds.
The beauty of its colored wings
expresses a joy that sings
a song of Life, just to be,
whose only purpose is to see
all God's creatures loved so much,
can live their lives with the butterfly touch.
As we travel our world from place to place,
we too can move with this butterfly grace.
Wherever we go, however we pray,
opens the way for a butterfly day.

DISCOVERING THE POET WITHIN

I know you are in there
hidden in the cobwebs of self-doubt.
Mental spiders weave their limitations
making me afraid to
step through the wispy curtain.
Like lint on dark cloth,
fear of failure
sticks to my intentions.

Putting pencil to paper,
the language of my soul
begins to speak itself into existence.
All the *I can'ts* and *what ifs*
blown away by winds of wonder.

Creating is my life.
I cannot die as long
as there is a poem within me.

HAPPINESS STEW

As soon as
A constant whine
Hoping gladness
Will then be mine
If only I hadn't
Another lament
Wishing to reverse
Some event

Is happiness
A future to long for
Or in a past where
I should close the door
What about the now
Sparkling with joy
No nagging thoughts
Compete to annoy

I need not advance
Nor retreat
Grass is the greenest
Under my feet
It's a special day
Whether sun or rain
How content I feel
No matter what pain

Living each moment
Always fresh and new
Gives me my own brand
Of happiness stew

AFTER THE STORM

she stands,
tall, stately, smiling.
A yellow halo
encircles her dark face,
an emblem of courage
withstanding the
harrowing hail and
conceited wind,
absorbed only in its own
momentum.

Around her,
battered crops
refuse to rise.

My sunflower refuses to fall.

ON MY WATCH

What fun it is to observe,
no obligation to reserve
personal opinions about what I see,
comparing events to what's happened to me.

Appreciation of what I perceive
lets me enjoy the moment to conceive
a peace that can dismiss some view
of what someone else ought to do.

How freeing it is not to judge
or give advice that ends in a grudge.
To watch with unbiased revelation
satisfies every life expectation.

LIFE CYCLE

I am seed

Reaching through the gristle of soil
I leave Mother Earth's womb
for the light of life

I am bud

Unfolding my petal wings
to fly high above dusty origin
A brushstroke of wind
nearly ends my smooth transition

I am flower

Perfuming the air waves with news
of birth marriage death
Even my wilting is gentle
like salt added to the flavor of life

I am seed

BREAKFAST AT J.C.'S

Each morning at my favorite café
I meet new companions
We silently eat our usual
breakfast of champions
Over newspapers
we'll notice each other awhile
then we usually speak
but sometimes just smile

Next comes conversation
that often begins
a new friendship which
hopefully never ends
Perhaps it's a short-term friend
flavor of the day
lasting a moment but
something tasty to say

This ever-expanding
family of mine
starts my day with no
recipe or outline
but joyous awakening
in a delicious way
to what truly nourishes
and is here to stay

FENCES

Are there fences in space?
What do they look like?
No astronaut has reported
an extra-terrestrial fence.
Even if made of brick or wood,
weightless still.

Maybe that capsule called a space ship
is a fence
keeping out elements of harm, protecting
the technology within.

That is what fences do,
give security from an outside world,
inside, keep us from straying.

Our earth fences are really thought forces,
telling the story of our lives.
The white picket fence, symbol
of family wholeness
or the sterile block wall, hiding
some industrial maze.
Over a backyard fence a tidbit of gossip.

The split rail fence of Abraham Lincoln fame,
a form of beauty in a harsh farm life.
Maybe a tiny rosebud entwines that
rough-hewn wood.
The future President picking such a
delicate flower,
holding it in gentle giant hands,
appreciates the moment,
lets go of all the mental fences
he is facing.

Fences begin and end as thinking.
Thought fences can either hem me in,
secure me, or expand into infinite space
where there are no limits.

Friends make my life sing. The rhythm of their lives touching mine is a symphony -- or at least a song. My friends were certainly there for me when I needed them.

I also heard from people I barely knew, as well as dear friends I hadn't seen in years. A large shopping bag overflowed with notes and caring cards. They meant everything to me at the time. I had intended to re-read them when I could and respond to the outpouring of love, but as the weeks passed, I felt burdened by that desire.

Finally, one day I realized those messages had become a symbol of tragedy. I knew that the love that had sent them needed no formal response. With great gratitude, I let them go -- unanswered. That was another door closed on the past, another opened to the present.

Even strangers became instant friends at the time of the accident. A young couple heading for a week-end vacation stopped on the freeway to offer assistance. On their way back three days later, they checked at the hospital to see how I was doing. I don't even know their names. I hope they read this and realize what their kindness meant to me.

Each friend brought their own lyrics to my need, but the following poem is dedicated to all of them.

You
know
who you are.
Thank
you.

BEST FRIENDS

Always there, my stick-like-glue friend,
dispersing your love without end.
Made-from-scratch meals brought to the door,
multitude offers to do something more.
A call to say you're thinking of me
unlocks the prison of misery.

I've shared the microcosm of my heart,
trusting your confidence before I start.
A healing giggle, often the thing
to lift my thought, take away the sting.
You are my ever friend, a loyal one
who shines on me as constant as the sun.

NAIL ART

Hovering over outstretched hand
she applies acrylic with artistic skill
A fingernail becomes the canvas
as smooth strokes of brush
bring forth her colorful painting
a soft Monet or vibrant Matisse

Chatter of Vietnamese
flutter of tiny bodies
energize the small shop
with bird-like industry

I watch my transformed nails
become long elegant
color of terra cotta

An ocean away
a country's greatest resource
silently sails
bringing dedication and design
to create my small masterpiece

MUSEUM MUSE

Alone in a museum
Surrounded by abstract art
What does it mean
Wouldn't the same design
Printed on fabric
Be fashionable
Frame it hang it
Resistance rises

I battle tradition
Landscape
Seascape
Still life
My virgin eyes
Examine every detail
Unveiled revelation speaks

Suddenly I am the canvas

Light from pallet
Of unknown source
Bathes my being
I am brushed with riotous color
Delicate forms
Soothe my painted senses
Expression of line
Elevates
Expands my portrait
Into gentle symbols
That incite peace

The painting becomes me

LIVING IN THE MOMENT

Life consumed with love, hope, joy
Expands like a favorite toy.

Dismissing fear that disturbs my peace
Helps that buoyant feeling increase.

What is this moment bringing to me?
Gratitude for good in all I see.

Each expression glimpsed for what it is,
A manifestation of what God gives.

The ancient truth, *Now is the accepted time,*
Gives serenity that can always be mine.

YOUR MOMENT

Now it is your turn. What are some special or even ordinary moments that you can immortalize in verse? You don't have to write a whole poem, perhaps just a line or two -- even a title that can be used later. I often do that. I have a whole page of titles that have come to me. I will gradually cross them off as I write the poem to match. However, I have been known to change them many times as the poem comes to life. It was the appellative, though, that gave birth to verse.

As you start thinking in poetry, be prepared to write instantly when an idea hits you, especially if you don't have your journal handy. I have used paper table mats, napkins, even the back of a check. One time in church, I used the collection envelope to jot down a line for a poem I had been working on. (Please don't tell anyone that.)

When I do serious writing and editing, I use a yellow legal pad, then transfer it to the computer for its final form. Why not try a title right now?

This
is your moment,
have fun!

TOUCHING

MEMORIES

Growing up, as I did, in a small farming community fosters both charming *and* challenging memories.

It was comforting for me to think and write about my personal history, recalling experiences fondly. I stayed away, for the most part, from any negative mental images that would tend to draw me down.

Writing about people and events in our past can be a forgiveness milestone. When we record an experience in poetry, it seems to take on a more objective view – almost as if we are writing about someone else. It is like standing across the room and watching ourselves. We become detached, less vulnerable and justifying.

I don't think we have to suffer to write creatively, but life experiences often bring out our compassionate side, forgiving others – and ourselves.

The imagery of our past
oils the wheels of moving verse.

LAVENDER LOVE

Hidden under a white box
of costume jewelry
I find it,
seventeen inches of lavender ribbon,
tattered, useless.

Memories are tied in lavender,
pigtails, ponytails, love letters.

First orchid,
the trembling hands of my date
pinning it to my shoulder,
afraid he would touch all
the wrong places.

Lilacs,
cascading against the back porch
atomize, encircle me
with each slam of the screen door.

Love smells like lavender.
Grandmother,
embracing me as a little girl
scented with her drug store perfume.

The gifts of my life,
re-wrapped
in a remnant of lavender.

AFTER THE RAIN

Huddled on the kitchen floor,
arms around my best friend,
his wet collie coat
leaves an imprint on my shirt.

Lightening unzips summer sky,
thunder vibrates Victorian farmhouse
trembling in sync with my heart.

Grandmother calmly shells peas
into the pan on her lap,
not seeming to notice the storm.
She looks up
smiles her love,
*After the rain you can take
a bath on the back porch.*

The round tin tub
for warm baths by the iron stove
humbly receives rain
so soft
it can barely be felt.

When the last drop
is wrung from the clouds,
I race to the porch
all fears forgotten.

Easing into the cool water,
my nine-year-old colt legs
slide up to my chin.

I giggle.
Outside, naked.
It's not even Saturday.

THE BLACK FLASH

Just a dog
big and black with yellow eyes
that look like two shiny over-easy eggs
peering from an iron skillet

Jack is a rounder
Life on the farm by the lake
filled with his specialty

Milking time
cow round-up
Squealing pigs need no coaxing
when Jack calls *sooie* with an *arf*

Harvest season
brings the dinner bell clang
Even farm hands well-rounded
with a bark or two

One day
the school bus
rounding a curve
slipped into the lake

Like a black arrow
Jack flew from the field
straight into the water
One by one he made his rounds
gently leading each child to safety

In these parts
Jack the rounder
now known as
The Barking Black Flash
we hope will always be around

MY CENTENARIAN MOTHER

(1898 -   )

Smooth skin contrasts with
curly wrinkles of her white hair.
Eyes pierce with inner vision
those who come into her presence.
Gentle response or spunky retort
asserts independence.

With tape recorder purring,
I probe this loved encyclopedia
filled with family information.

Living in three centuries,
her world expands
from horses to jets
from wood stove to microwave.

Homesteading a section of land
for his thirteen children,
her great-grandfather
the root of *my* tree
was as sturdy as the fields
he plowed and planted.

A card game played in the
light of smoking kerosene lamps,
their TV of the time.
Sleigh rides to town in winter
when wagons could not conquer snow,
their space adventure.

A quilt created with spinster aunt
now displayed on my daughter's wall,
its tiny stitches and patriotic colors
sew a design of museum quality.

Baseball, always her passion,
fills summer hours.
One hundred year old ears now
pressed to the radio hear every play
while cheering *her* St. Louis Cardinals
with unyielding loyalty.

The forms in her life,
family, friends, farm
shaped by an unfolding America,
represent the best of a nation.

My mother lives on into a third century
ever greening her life with growth,
demonstrating eternal being.

HEADLINE: Anniversary
Of Landing on Iwo Jima

My brother, my protector, my hero.
From Guadalcanal to Iwo Jima,
fighting battle after battle.

I read every letter,
study pictures of tropical islands
with bare chested, dog-tagged,
rifle-in-hand young men.
Places never imagined from
Midwestern farm lands.

Each picture shows fading youth,
accelerated manhood.
At home, my eleven-year-old eye views change,
twelve, thirteen, fourteen-year-old wisdom.

Witness historic flag raising on Iwo Jima,
the battles are over.
Warm family homecoming.
Questions...reluctant answers.

Marine uniform with new gold bars,
handsome officer. Saluted.
How proud I am.

Still my big brother
now protecting his teen-age sister.
Approves my dates,
shares his car,
always there.

He lost his last battle.
Cigarettes, government issue,
finally took from me
what enemy bullets had failed to do.

My brother, my hero.

MILKING TIME

Four A.M.
Grandfather's hands
move to the rhythm
of an inner orchestra
Years of practice
leave a touch
gentle as the animal
relieved of its precious cargo

Her chewing cud and swishing tail
generate warmth within
the frigid stall
Kerosene lanterns splinter light
through the cracks of fading red barn

An untamed cat hungrily cries
from the shadows
With changeless momentum
Grandfather shoots a stream of milk
into its tiny mewing mouth

Picking up the pail
he heads for the farm house
Warm milk over warm oatmeal
waiting

BRISCOE LANDMARK

The buzz saw spins its teeth
through a hundred years of
oak legend.

How many generations
circle her trunk?
How many swings have
hung from loyal branches?
How many children
played in her shade?

A one room school house
planted on Briscoe farmland
ripened on her roots,
replaced long ago
by great-grandson's
contemporary cottage.

Now stripped of life by lightning,
our lopsided oak
accepts her fate.
Firewood.

I knew I was healed when I was able to write this poem about my husband who passed on several years ago. Up until this point, I would have felt too sad, but with the objectivity of poetry, it became a purely creative joy.

Poetry should speak for itself. In this one, however, several in our critique group did not understand it until I changed the word "you" to "him." Which do you prefer?

Who are the "pearls" in your life? Could you compose something that would convey your feelings?

Composing poetry with passion
can be a regenerating and healing means
for anyone facing adversity.

THE PEARL ON MY PILLOW

I watch him sleeping

Sands of time
Have enhanced his luster
Refined character
Whitened his crown
Removed the shell
Left him with me to
Jewel my life

I wear him proudly

AM I IRISH

Do I have smiling Irish eyes?
How do eyes smile?
I look in the mirror and laugh,
Green eyes grin back.

I must be Irish

Do I love green?
Summer's full foliage,
Tree trunks veneered in
Emerald islands of moss,
Children rolling down hills
Of velvet jade,
I see green everywhere.

I must be Irish

Do I know a Shamrock?
Wading through river of clover
I inhale its sweet breath,
Feel its gentle presence.
More than a national emblem.

I must be Irish

Do I have Irish ancestors?
Leprechaun stories of
Flynn, Holt, Kelly,
Roam in the crevice of my memory.

I must be Irish

Do I love St. Patrick's Day?
More than a *wee* bit.

I *must* be Irish

YOUR MEMORIES

What about your own memories? Have any of my poems reminded you of similar experiences or relationships? Did you have a teacher or relative that especially inspired you? You might want to write about one of them and use their name as the title. Remember, I called the poem of the oak tree by a proper name because it originally belonged to my great-grandfather.

Listening is a powerful tool in writing, not only listening to people and sounds around us, but to that inner voice that often has a lot to say when we are quiet. Unable to be physically active for so long caused me to listen more actively. I found myself expressing things I didn't know I knew. I would often end up with a metaphor that I hadn't planned or charming sound-alike words without even meaning to. This is the delight of creating. You realize you are not *doing* it, but just *being* it.

> The camera of the present
> takes pictures
> of the past

> or

> The camera of the past
> takes pictures
> of the present

SOCIAL ISSUES

THAT

TOUCH

ME

Empathy for others is important to me. Strong opinions mellow as I write poetically about social situations.

Some years ago I attended workshops that had a great impact on me, both politically and socially. Before the group took a position on any national issue, we had to do research and be able to debate every side. What an education in seeing another point of view!

Poetry has done that for me as well. To write from the standpoint of someone or something else is to gain not only a new outlook but also original poetry. I've written as a seed, bud, and flower in "Life Cycle." I am Mona Lisa being painted by Leonardo di Vinci. I am an abstract canvas in "Museum Muse." I am a fish in "Life from a Fish Bowl." The choices are endless.

When I spoke to a first grade class about poetry, I offered to help a six year old girl with her three line poem. She was going to write *about* something, so I suggested she write *as* something. I asked her questions to bring out her creative talent. What do you want to be? *A flower.* What kind? *A rose.* What color? *Red.* What do you have for arms? *Petals.* What do you do with them? *Hold them out and think of you!* Here is the result:

I am a rose of red
I open my petal arms
And think of you

What a rich resource for recovery – to be so involved in thinking from a whole new perspective that we *become* imaginative verse.

RECOURSE

Sometimes I start at the top
      pull strings
            brave the brass
                  to gain the gold

Sometimes I begin at the bottom
      work my way up
            through tin links
                 to settle for silver

As I pray my way
      through an entrenched
            chain of command
                 I test my mettle

THE SEED

Prisoners file into the makeshift chapel,
a double-wide trailer, drab but clean.
All look alike in orange coveralls
but within, range from confused to mean.

Faces tell of their wasted lives.
Bowing shaved heads in remorse,
the freedom they want so much
now controlled by a larger force.

Some hear the Bible Lesson with respect,
others listen through mild contempt.
Motives as varied as the men themselves,
govern their struggling attempt.

The Chaplain wonders, *Is this all worth while?*
Then some macho inmate wipes away a tear,
unable to find the words
for what he's glimpsed has overcome his fear.

Great reward fills this sacred hour,
helping someone in their need.
Marching back to a dingy cell,
they've been touched by a tiny seed.

SHADES OF SUMMER 1956

That summer in Little Rock
Black and white issues
Become newly gray
When rights of black
Traditions of white
Seen in new color

Vibrant hues of equality
Varnished my teens with
Shared classes football games
White cheered black
Black cheered white in
U of I orange and blue

Scenes of segregation
stir my naive youth
How could they
What can I say

I quiz my host
Argue accuse
In charming condescension
He responds
You northern girls don't understand

Short distance from my roots
Million miles of culture change
Color me understanding

TALK TO ME

A remnant of history
rests in the palm of my hand
holding untold stories,
impossible to tell.

Talk to me, Berlin wall.

Your face of crumbling cement,
pox marked from bullet wounds,
stained by graffiti -- or blood,
speechless.

How many cigarette smoking
soldiers lounged at your feet?
Were you wet with the sweat of
fear filled young deserters
climbing their way to freedom?
Did you feel the pain of
keeping in and keeping out
those who worship liberty?

As you crumbled beneath
the passion of people who
tore you apart with bare hands,
did I hear you breathe
a sigh of relief?

Talk to me....

TEEN MAFIA

Before

Crazy geek wears a trench coat to school
Stupid jock thinks he's so cool
Popularity is important to me
Why do I care what they think or see

After

How can we bridge the gap in our view
Value each other in what we do
We meet half-way
I hold my hand out to you

Princess Diana was killed shortly after my own accident, so her passing was especially distressing for me. It felt like a personal blow, although what I was learning about the eternal nature of Life sustained me.

This poem came much later and helped to convey my feelings. It was hard not to accuse and blame those involved in her death. That was why I changed meter and turned the last stanza into a question, which is what I have learned to do when tempted to tell the reader how to think. It can also be effective to use the first line for a title as I did here.

Although it may appear to be a light touch for so sensitive a subject, I was going for the "rap" sound that often has controversial content.

It could even be read
with a funereal cadence.

CANNIBALS

Lie in wait
Stalk their prey
Foster hate

Hide in dark
Flash bulbs light
Cameras click
Through the night

Sighting Di
In her car
Lick their lips
Follow star

Is the way to
Stop this caper
Refuse to buy
Sleazy paper

I call the following untitled verse an "anger poem," something written to release that known poison. It is what I encourage teen-agers to do rather than resort to violence.

I would like to see them turn to prayer but have come to see that

poetry
is a form of prayer.

UNTITLED

He attacks me with his
polluting intellectualism.
I am bombarded, raped
with haughty words
meant to belittle, wound.

Building up his own self-esteem
by tearing down mine,
I witness the control technique
used by little people
with giant egos.

My local tyrant,
whose practiced body language
skillfully shifts,
waits for my response.
His cat and mouse game,
charming to cruel to charming
plays itself out.
I don't take the bait.

Throughout the centuries,
how many Herods and Hitlers
have mimicked greatness
with this mesmerism
of manipulation?

Doesn't love,
the measure of true nobility,
impress
with humility?

DESERT WINDMILLS

The three arms of
        silver giants
twirl to the dance
        of invisible force

Towers of power
        mill their energy
into the swing of life

I flick a switch
        and am grateful

THEY SAY....

My lifted eyebrows,
lowered voice,
sleek confidentiality,
implied self-importance --

shattered.

Who says?
Who are they?

I hate it when Dad
calls my bluff.

This is a true story about a friend of mine who overcame his adversities through acting out the written word. He was selective about his roles. I quickly learned the importance of metaphors and similes in painting my word pictures. They are the two main figures of speech. I used the metaphor of snow to describe the actor's dilemma in choosing scripts.

For me,
poetry
has to have hope.

It is what carried me through the whole recovery period and continues today.

THE ACTOR

Pages of script
fall to the floor in white mounds
Specks of type
like soot covering snow
buried in an avalanche
of frustration

Another role to reject
whose hopeless characters
are unworthy of snowballing career

He picks up final manuscript
The Life of Robert Lewis Stevenson
a man of courage
dying of consumption

Drifts of insight
melt frozen resolve

Maybe I could cough with hope

I usually write about my own life experiences, but in this poem I address the challenge of broken relationships with a totally made up scenario. For those who might be recovering from just such a break-up, however, both the message and the style might be helpful.

I was also experimenting with rhyming the first and third, second and fourth lines.

"Truth in poetry"
means it must ring true
even if imaginary.

LIGHT AT THE END

He walks out the door suitcase in hand

I sink to my knees in utter despair

Twist off my wedding band

Try desperately not to care

Looking through the window pane

First rays of dawn feast on the night

I may never be the same

But *no one* can take away my light

SEPARATE CHECKS

It had always been done for me.
My dad, boyfriends, husband,
quietly picking up that mysterious ticket
placed by gum chewing waitress or
black-coated waiter
depending on where we were,
whom I was with.

Daddy talked to them all.
By the time we left
their life stories lay on our plates,
an unmerited tip on the table.

Boyfriends, too shy to banter,
memorized the tablecloth
as server approached with
our exit paper.

I watched my husband grow in competence
as he paid check after check.
Always generous,
even while straining our budget muscle,
he learned the procedure well.

Then there was
no daddy, no boyfriends, no husband.
Only women, women, women.

Initiation Day with the girls,
it lies there like a leper we are
afraid to touch.
Finally, I open the leather folder,
numbers neatly score various tastes.
What do I do now?
I rest my credit card on the leprous garment.

Protests around the table,
Let's split it.
But you had dessert.
You had a drink and I didn't.
Everyone figure out what they owe.

Is this the way the feminine game is played?
Next time, I'll not go for the gold.
Separate checks, please.

In the next poem, I am poking a little fun at my world-class resort community -- and at myself for wanting to close the doors of Paradise.

This very same spot seemed a dismal place from a wheelchair until I began to write my heart out. I have found that self-absorption is self-defeating. That is why thinking and writing about ideas, words, phrases, stanzas, and finally whole poems became important to my recovery. It took thought off me and onto the bigger picture.

Now,
as I walk freely around my desert oasis,
I love the action.

EVERYONE WANTS TO BE THE LAST PERSON IN PARADISE

Too many people,
too much traffic
interrupt my paradise,
hiccups the desert day.

Pets people their way
through visiting crowds, while
people snarl their five-o'clock growl
sniffing tail lights, starting fights.

Sand dunes give way
to sand traps as
waves of green drown
age-old Joshua trees.
Is our village Barbie dolling
its way to Glitzville?

As another wagon load arrives,
I want to close ranks,
circle the troops.
Can't they find
their own paradise?

I've got mine.

YOUR SOCIAL STATEMENT

What a great opportunity you have now! You can express all your private opinions, criticisms, annoyances, or even approval in verse and call it a creative art form. Some of our deeply held social and political views written in poetry can take on a gentler tone and seem less strident. One of the rules we have in our poetry group is that we are not allowed to critique the content, only the style.

When a stanza begins to sermonize (on its own, of course) I turn it into a question as I mentioned about "Cannibals." Then readers can decide for themselves how to view the topic. Some of my subjects could be called controversial, but that was the way I saw them. Sometimes it is helpful to let even negative feelings surface.

I wrote poetry for almost three years before I had the courage to write my "anger poem." I must admit that it felt good since it was a composite of several encounters I have had over the years. Seeing our thoughts on paper just might show us the way to healing, if that is what is needed.

Remember,
it is your choice
whether to share or not.

A GAME

OF

WORD TOUCH

A useful exercise in our poetry group is for one person to choose several unrelated words and then for all of us to create a poem using those words in some form.

It is thoroughly enjoyable and is one of the best things I do. I have no idea how I do it, except to have a subject in mind and use the words to bring it forth. Or, occasionally a word will stand out and inspire an idea, like "aspen," which led me to "The Buds of Columbine."

In that poem notice all the words with "s" in them, which is alliteration -- repetition of an initial sound. The title, "Lavender Love," is another example. I enjoy the lyrical ring of alliteration so you will find it throughout my narrative, as well as my poems. You probably know this intuitively, but being consciously aware of its use makes for better poetry.

I had to learn to be alone again after many weeks of full-time help, so inventing poetry with selected words was playful amusement. Another plus for creative writing, at least for me, is its solitary nature -- an avocation you can enjoy anytime, anyplace -- alone.

How many wasted moments have been spent waiting? Now, I always have a poem in progress, so that helps keep me calm and patient. Or sometimes, I write about where I am and what is going on.

Life
gives us
infinite opportunities.

THE BUDS OF COLUMBINE

The crackle of guns
falling bodies of students
on the threshold of life
seen in slow motion
as two teens
worshipping at the shrine of violence
become a jury to their peers

In the distance
budding Colorado aspens
withstand the freezing snow
as does a country
who mourns her youth

(falling, crackle, threshold,
shrine, jury, aspen, distance)

A LOCAL'S OATH

Thirty-five miles an hour
in a fifty mile zone,
he drives down one-eleven
in the narrow hallway
of aging self-absorption.

The pollen of my anger
cascades over me,
twisting my patience
into the unspoken gossip
of annoyance.

Sour sweetens
as I remember
the margin in our ages.
Someday,
must I give full refund
for every time I rabbited
around a visiting tortoise?

There, but for the law --
or lie of time,
go I.

(cascade, gossip, refund, pollen,
sour, margin, hallway, twist)

The next two poems use the same seven words, but have an entirely different flavor. This is an inventive method that never fails to inspire me -- and I am always amazed at the results.

<u>WORDS</u>:
flat
carpet
waste
rinsed
tube
loop
fingernail

When I discovered it was the author's choice whether or not to use punctuation, I felt daring in my first try without it. Some of the poetry greats have used infinite variation in punctuation, capitalization, and enjambment – the running of one line onto the next. It seemed like a maze at first, but I soon began to enjoy the twists and turns. I believe it is called "style," and most authors develop their own. In the final metaphor, however, the only one who has to love your poem is you (and maybe your mother).

77

DESERT MOURNING

The crunch of my hiking boots
only sound as I walk
over flat carpet of sand

This desert wasteland
rinsed in stillness
quiets my grieving thoughts

I rest in the shade of a cactus
whose tall tube loops its prickly
fingernails around itself

Healing solace

THOUGHTS OF AN OSCAR NOMINEE

This can't be real.
Am I finally at the Academy Awards?
That whole scene
red carpet
screaming fans
microphones in my face
rinsed with an aura of unreality.

Can't breathe in this pink
tube of a dress.
Makes my breasts look as flat
as the tires on my pastel Porsch.
Hope Ralph is watching.

I want to bite my fingernails.
Sitting between famous parents
beautiful Mother
director Father
finally in the loop on my own.
I dare not waste this opportunity
to make them proud.

And the winner is
Gwyneth Paltrow.

Another assignment was to write a poem from a picture of our choice. A watercolor of a young woman looking out the window, obviously waiting for someone, was the backdrop for this next poem with its jocular insinuations.

In my opinion, pictures and poetry can compliment each other. Someone gave me a book of nature poems by Robert Frost, illustrated with magnificent seasonal photographs. What breath-taking inspiration! I haven't done it yet, but to poeticize an actual antique photograph is one of my goals.

Reading poetry was something I had to do in high school and college as an assignment, but it wasn't until I began to write it myself, that I actually learned to enjoy reading the works of poets of the past and the present.

To be open to a new cultural experience often helps regenerate and expand our lives. Someone who has never read poetry might find it stimulating and even therapeutic. When we are recovering from any physical or emotional problem, change of thinking and outlook may be a necessity. Our past attitudes may no longer be relevant to our present growth. I am happy to say that my life is constantly in transition.

The only thing
that stays the same
is change.

WAITING

Where in the world could he possibly be
Promised faithfully to be home by three
My friends are expecting Jimmy and me

Waiting is such an arduous task
Keeping hands busy is just a mask
For anxious feelings I hope won't last

Has he stopped to see the bitch down the street
She acts to me like a menace in heat
My hands start shaking my heart leaps a beat

I look through the window for the hundredth time
There they are the playful dog with that son of mine
Just what you would expect from a boy of nine

TIRING*

Driving along Pacific Coast Highway
between <u>sheer</u> cliffs of Palisades
and setting sun on the ocean,
each wave blinks like orange <u>hazard</u> lights.

My wife with the rhythm of a <u>type</u>writer
drones out her continual gossip column.
My head bobs half listening.
I wish she would stop the chatter
to enjoy the seascape.

Instead she opens a can of <u>nuts,</u>
crunching as she feeds her ego
with conversation about herself.

How I would love to <u>reverse</u> that
glowing ball on the horizon
to the moment I <u>agreed</u>
to this trip.

I should have known
she was the <u>nail</u> in the tire
that would make my vacation flat
or reach the point
where I would blow out
all the pent-up resentment
from years of petty annoyances.

(*This is a tongue-in-cheek play on our seven chosen
words. I underlined them here for clarity.)

YOUR WORDS

"Show, don't tell" is the axiom of poetry. Painting pictures with words is the brushstroke that impacts good writing. I didn't know what this meant until I had written several poems *telling* how beautiful something was, or how inspiring or happy or whatever. Our poetry workshop leader encouraged me to *show* with words, not *tell*. I finally got it! I rewrote "Museum Muse" many times before I metaphorically became the canvas and let abstract art paint my portrait. That was the epiphany, or awakening, that took me out of my attempts to tell about my revelation and instead showed how it felt to *be* the painting. It was thrilling for me to see this idea unfold on the page. Then I saw the difference. I still make the mistake occasionally, but now I can catch it more readily.

You might want to try some of the words our group used when you create your next poem. Or I will give you seven new ones: tablecloth, glass, hair, door, smile, rock, future.

Now you know
how the game is played,
so enjoy!

A TOUCH

OF

TRAVEL

Travel is an expansive topic, even if it is only across town. "The House on the Corner" came from driving down a local street. During the months I was unable to travel, sometimes even to the dinner table, writing about my previous trips to France and Italy was an adventure in itself.

I found unlimited space travel in thinking about the infinite nature of Spirit. In my mind there wasn't a place I couldn't go. That is why poetry was the perfect outlet for my imagination to roam. It was also my weapon in the battle with boredom. You cannot help being inspired with your own compelling poetry.

My travel poems taught me the importance of research in order to write with authority. Although I had been to Venice, I didn't know much about its history or culture. When I wanted to share my gondola ride in "Queen of the Adriatic," I had to go to the encyclopedia and learn more about that sinking city.

Think about your own journeys in life. Where have they taken you? What did you learn? Put a few words on paper or the computer and see where they lead. It is surprising how simple it is to get started.

You may find yourself
traveling
at the speed of Light.

THE HOUSE ON THE CORNER

Perfectly painted
sand beige,
soil brown.
Lawn of desert heritage
gives way to grass so
emerald green and pedicured,
I want to sink my bare toes
into its Irish roots.

Flowers
born
of hot house climate
chant their diversity,
pick me,
pick me.

The book jacket exterior
reads
like a biography
of people within.
The quality of their lives
reflected
in the scene of serenity
whispers
pages of peace.

QUEEN OF THE ADRIATIC

An aria from Puccini floats across the water
as our gondola walks the streets of Venice.
The Italian tenor,
unmoved by water spraying
into one-oared opera house,
brushes the keys of his accordion
with the artistry of Michelangelo
painting his angels.

Musical notes rise and fall with the Adriatic tide,
seeping into cracks of sinking structures
built from Byzantine to Renaissance,
for conquering and conquered.
We canal our way through this city of antiquity
under its curved and carved bridges.
The musty smell of aging buildings
shares the air with operatic sound
that hints of a dying love.

In the last act,
Venice will *not* abdicate her throne
for a final curtain call.

HEADS UP

A puff of clouds move across
the Italian sky
above St. Mark's Square
The soot covered Cathedral
gives no hint
of the magnificent mosaics
that clutter the interior

Lovers toss coins into a fountain
an up-side-down umbrella
ornately carved
Agile pigeons
startled by our approach
flutter upward
leaving a portion of their lunch

on our heads

SEARCH FOR HEMINGWAY

Lost in the miracle of Paris
surrounded by the language of
poets and artists
I sponge its culture into mine

To sit in his chair
soak up invisible words
spoken at his table
gathering greatness
would make bells toll

Wandering the Left Bank
I choose a small café
lunch and listen
Through the symphonic
sounds of French
I hear a whisper
You do know this was Hemingway's hangout

I'm home

THE TRAVELER

As I roam the world of life
A gentle nature stilling strife
Cultures encountered with respect
Are honored for each aspect

What will I find that is not in my thought
I take me along with each venture sought
Carry criticism that's what I'll find
Pack my love that is what will bind

No *ugly American* to judge or compare
But one who finds beauty everywhere
Kindred spirits wherever we are
My passport home no matter how far

When I travel -- or when I don't -- eating out is my favorite adventure. Most of my poems have been written while sitting at "my" table in a small café. The darling couple who own it have become like family to me since I have eaten breakfast there for several years. The first place I went on my maiden voyage in a wheelchair was to J.C.'s Patio Café. They had a table reserved for me with a big sign that read, "Welcome back, Dessa!" Many of the regulars whom I had met over meals sent me thoughtful messages after the accident.

It was here that my poetry journey began and became a highway of inspiration. Because poetry is observational, many ideas have come from this lively spot. One of my early poems was "Breakfast At J.C.'s," which describes perfectly why I am drawn to this friendly mental atmosphere. The poem hangs on their wall.

My latest fantasy is to return to Paris, find Hemingway's special café again, sit at his table, and write a poem. Talk about bells tolling!

You do not have to travel an inch to write your travel poem.

Start your engine
of inspiration
NOW.

THE

SPIRITUAL

TOUCH

I greatly appreciate the necessary physical care I received at Desert Regional Medical Center, Palm Springs, California. The dedicated doctors, nurses, and aides were expert and gentle in their professional service.

I feel, however, that my full recovery came as a result of spiritual awakening. Years of working as a practitioner in my church and serving as a chaplain in two county jails had already convinced me of the power of prayer.

Praying for myself as best I could, I was also grateful to my fellow church members, who were diligent in their prayerful support. One particular friend talked with me every day. Her love and pure spiritual understanding were essential to my progress. The more clearly I saw my spiritual identity, the more nearly the physical condition came into line with healing.

Occasionally, when I was discouraged, one of my friends would come immediately and talk or read to me. I remember one time, the friend who came in answer to my call shared something she had read just that day. It was exactly what I needed to hear.

There were many others, some I barely knew, who told me later that they held me in their prayers. One of the nurses literally held me in her arms and prayed during a dire moment. So many dear people of many different denominations and nationalities came to be a part of my healing.

After I was home, the nurse who visited daily to bandage a wound said, "Every time I leave here I feel I have witnessed a miracle." I felt blessed and grateful – and still do.

INFINITY

The allness of God encircles with love,

inside, outside, below and above.

Are objects *out there* in some place

or pure thoughts filling all space?

Infinite means no beginning or end,

no starting or stopping again and again.

Could Infinity ever be less

than a design made only to bless?

SONG AND DANCE MAN

Man, the action of what Love brings,

moving with freedom swings and sings

praises to a Cause wholly pure,

whose healing effects, I trust endure.

Rhythm of ideas dance joyous rounds,

flowing as one make glorious sounds.

ETERNITY

What is the millennium?
A measure of time?
What is time?
A meaningless concept?
Time may fly or stand still, but
crossing over a digit
leaves no effect.
A birthday cannot change my identity.

Will the year two thousand
take away my breath or
breathe new life into me?
All the superstition
that goes with a number
pales before the infinite nature
of the universe
where time is swallowed up in eternity.

FROM TOP TO BOTTOM

God includes all space and time
My starting point and bottom line
No other premise has beginning
No other power is sustaining

Every conclusion ends the same
No one and no thing to blame
Love is saying *all is Mine*
Man is reflecting *all is Thine*

THE CHOICE

Slowness is beauty, Rodin has said.

Haste makes waste, I have also read.

Which shall I choose that clearly shows

quiet reflection of what God knows?

There is happily only one choice

when I listen and obey His voice.

I hear the answer and rejoice.

When there is some tragedy in the world, I feel the need to write a poem in response. It makes me feel I am helping to alleviate the pain of others as well as my own.

Dedicated
to
John F. Kennedy, Jr.

The Salute That Cannot Die

That image
carved in the soul of America
lives on
to inspire with courageous innocence
those who face deep waters

A little boy
climbing the ladder to manhood
in a political dynasty
lived life at one
yet apart
with glamorous grace

Now without barrier of time
he is forever saluting
his *heavenly* Father

WHAT SPOT

We were taught as a tiny tot
There is no spot where God is not
He is All and fills this space
Where is the evil to erase

If we see a spot to fear
Only claiming to be here
And ask Him about the blot
We hear the answer *What spot*

PURE LIGHT

Man the shine of spiritual light
Sees no shadow within his sight
Dazzling power asserts this right

Shining as one with light so pure
He radiates being secure
Reflecting ideas that endure

Man never doubts his brilliant Source
Illuminating that bright Force
Makes him glow always on course

This was one of my first attempts, both to journal comforting ideas and to rhyme. As a beginner, there was something about rhyming that made me feel like I was actually writing a poem – and it was fun. At least it got my thoughts off myself for five minutes which was remarkable at that early stage. I just started affirming everything I had ever heard about the nature of God that I felt must be true. So many of the "truths" I had thought and read over the years and, to some degree, proved for myself and others came pouring out on paper. I was amazed at the pencil in my hand and what it was writing on its own – or so it seemed.

Why
don't you let your
pencil speak
and see what it says?

The presence of God

Fills all space
Loves this place
Shines in every face
Moves at perfect pace

The presence of God

Healthy and secure
Powerful to insure
All that is pure
Needing no cure

The presence of God

Discerning and perceiving
Understanding and seeing
Supplying and receiving
Expressing all being

POINT OF VIEW

One God one Mind one view
The same for me and for you

Viewpoints have at least two
Conflicting in what to do

Decisions of One who knows all
Makes a unanimous call

From His vantage point I can never fall
When I live with no argument wall

YOUR SPIRITUAL POEM

Many of my early poems were of a spiritual nature. These may not be my best literary work, but they speak of deep insights that were helpful at the time. You, too, can feel at ease in writing about your innermost thoughts and trust your readers to interpret according to their own need. Their acceptance or rejection need not affect your convictions.

We often hesitate to open ourselves to others. I have certainly had to deal with that in writing about my recovery. I've always been quite candid about my life, but this new exposure takes it to the outer limits. Poetry is such a personal medium of expression that our words show exactly who we are and what we think. Most of us don't want to do that. Perhaps it is because we are afraid that we will be judged by others. That has been one of the biggest healings to come out of this experience. I am no longer concerned (most of the time) with what others think of me or what I should or should not do. How freeing! Many of us are raised to the tune of, "What will the neighbors think?" -- or family?" -- or friends?" I believe self-esteem comes when we listen to a Higher Power -- or inner voice or whatever we call it -- and do what our spiritual intuition tells us to do. Then, it will be what is right for *us*.

That would make a great poem.
Do you want to start
or shall I?

SOMETIMES

I NEED A

TOUCH OF

SILLY

My humor, sometimes called silly, carried me through devastating times. When I awoke after the accident, unable to speak, I was handed a yellow pad and wrote, *We have got to quit meeting like this.* That crazy gesture was comforting to my family and friends, who then knew the one they loved was in there somewhere.

I think the people I admire the most are the ones who can laugh at themselves and find humor in just about anything. When my husband died, my daughter and I would talk on the phone many times a day, comforting each other. We would end every conversation with, "Other than that Mrs. Lincoln, how did you like the play?" That sounds terribly insensitive now as I look at it on paper, but at the time, the stupidity of it made us laugh and we were consoled.

My dear friend, Shannon Peck, co-author with her husband Scott in their book, *Liberating Your Magnificence: 25 Keys to Loving & Healing Yourself,* tells the story of our friendship of love and laughter. For twenty years she and I have giggled our way through some pretty challenging experiences. She shares how the spiritual quality of joy brings healing.

That is why I love laughter.
It brings joy,
just as joy brings laughter.

I now speak easily but feel I have found my true voice in writing.

THOUGHTS OF MONA LISA
WHILE BEING PAINTED
BY LEONARDO DI VINCI

Hurry up Leo, I must get home to fix supper.

What feast shall I prepare?
Roast duck, tortellini?

So bored,
motionless for hours,
asleep all over.
Wiggle toes, waggle fingers,
grin.

If only I knew how to read.
I love words spoken by poets,
songs sung by minstrels.
To read would make them mine.
Women are kept in such ignorance.
I may never govern,
even allowed an opinion
but not read, why?

Leonardo is an attractive man.
I wonder if....
Mona...stop....

Why is he so slow?
Never thought a portrait took this long,
only a birthday present.

Leo, please hurry. No one
will see this except my husband.

CALIFORNIA COOL

With you I am everything

You are strawberry in yogurt

The nutmeg on latte

You are tofu in my salad

Equal to decaf

You bring Th'i to my Chi

Yin to my Yang

Without you I am only half hip

WINTER SNOB

The white Egret
Elegant in posture and wingspread
Meant to soar through mist
Over mountains
Under bridges
Leaves a jet stream of mystery

Winter lounging on the tenth tee
She becomes
Just another snow bird
Beak lowers
Snobbery melts
She grins and walks away

When my life changed so drastically, I received a great deal of uninvited input. I realized how often we try to tell each other what to do. The words *you should* are now being eliminated (hopefully) from my vocabulary.

My goal
is just *to be*
and let others do the same.

YOU SHOULD

Why do we feel so inclined
to give advice all the time?

If I go to Paris, I'm told I must see Rome,
while another suggests I just stay home.

When I select a movie I would like to see,
film critic friends say it's too sad for me.

Are you going to wear that color,
really means, you should choose another.

Is every decision up for review,
telling each other what to do?

There is one thing *you* should know.
Let me decide, I'll reap what I sow.

LIFE FROM A FISH BOWL

I wrap myself in my liquid coat,
whose warp and woof,
snuggle me
in weightless texture.

Watching the world
from my glass house,
strange amphibians
swish by its windows,
buoyant with hope
or sinking in despair.

They wiggle their bodies
in and out of clothes,
embrace each other --
or point fins,
laugh and cry.
A minnow appears
another disappears.

Life drifts by....

THE ELEPHANT IN THE DOORWAY

How will I know what to do
When I don't have a clue
Which choice could be true

I listen and hear You say
This is clearly My way
Like an elephant in a doorway

Direction comes all the time
God's love keeps me in line
How could I miss my jumbo sign

YOUR HUMOR

My daughter recounts many hilarious things I did and said during some of my not-too-coherent moments. It has become a family joke, and I love that we can tease about it. It does not offend me in the least. I am just glad that playfulness is so much a part of my nature, that it is there when I need it the most. Writing funny or even silly poetry has given me some of my happiest hours. I admire those who do it well. Dramatic, sensitive poetry is a true art, but being able to write clever humor takes not only great wit but immense humility, since we are often laughing at ourselves as well as one another.

What is the funniest thing you have ever witnessed? What is silly about yourself, whether you can admit it to anyone else or not? Why not write it down in short sentences and see what comes out? Laugh at it, then tear it up. At least you have a beginning for humorous poetry. (Notice, I am not saying, *you should.*)

I wish you
all the joy
that you can wish.

William Shakespeare
Merchant of Venice

ONE LAST TOUCH

This book has been as much about overcoming adversity as about poetry. Writing was the vehicle in which I made my journey. You have been word-watching an emerging poet, who is still a work in progress.

The young trainer who helped me learn to walk again said, "I have never seen anyone come so far, so fast, and with such determination as you." In retrospect, I see this, not as human effort or will, but the gentle nudge of the divine presence -- what I call the *butterfly touch.* To touch each other's lives with this gentleness can only bless our universe -- our "one song."

My hope is that you will discover *your* world of lyrical, imaginative poetry that lies within. My discovery came in the blackest hour and has led to the lightest of days.

Please,
pass on the touch.

ABOUT THE AUTHOR

Dessa Byrd Reed was born in Charleston, Illinois and attended University of Illinois and Eastern Illinois University. She and her late husband moved to California many years ago. She has had several careers – homemaker, advertising representative for an international daily newspaper, interior designer, practitioner for her church, and chaplain in two county jails.

After seeing the benefits of writing poetry in her own recovery, she now speaks to groups, helping others find inspiration and direction in writing their verse. She also sponsors poetry contests in local high schools to encourage young people to communicate their feelings.

Deer Publishing
PMB # 164
74924 Country Club Drive #150
Palm Desert, California 92260
Fax: 760-345-4666 E-mail: DessaReed@aol.com
www.dessabyrdreed.com

on the road again